The Body in Action

Seeing

Claire Llewellyn

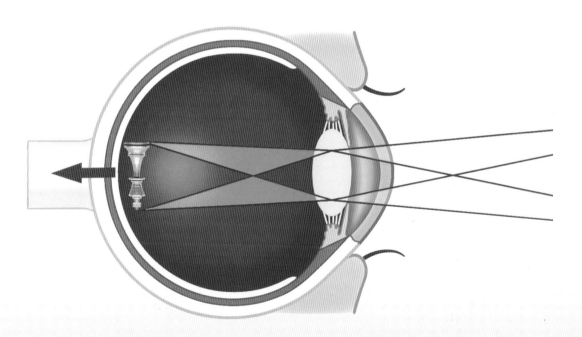

Titles in this series:
Eating
Moving
Seeing
Thinking and Feeling

Copyright © 2004 Bailey Publishing
Associates Ltd

Produced for A & C Black by
Bailey Publishing Associates Ltd
11a Woodlands
Hove BN3 6TJ

Editor: Alex Woolf
Designer: Stonecastle Graphics
Artwork: Michael Courtney
Cartoons: Peter Bull
Picture research and commissioned
photography: Ilumi Image Research
Consultant: Dr Kate Barnes

First published in 2004 by
A & C Black Publishers Ltd, 37 Soho Square,
London W1D 3QZ
www.acblack.com

British Library Cataloguing in Publication Data

ISBN 0 7136 63383

A & C Black uses paper produced with elemental
chlorine-free pulp, harvested from managed
sustainable forests.

Printed in Hong Kong
by Wing King Tong.

Picture Acknowledgements:
Corbis: Ariel Skeller: 5b; **Getty Images:**
Desmond Burdon: 23, Peter Cade: 16, Pascal
Crapet: 5t, Bruce Laurance: 4, Ryan McVay: 22,
Mark Romanelli: 12, Harry Sieplinga. HMS
Images: 18, Adam Smith: 28, Howard Sokol:
29, V.C.L: 20, 24, Nick White: 8; **Zul Mukhida:**
10; **Photofusion:** 26; **Popperfoto:** Gary
Payton: 14; **John Walmsley Education
Photos:** 27t.

Contents

Seeing is believing

YOU USE your sight more than any of your other **senses**. Your eyes help you to take in all sorts of information, such as colours, movement, light and dark. They allow you to see words and pictures, and they enable you to recognize the faces of your family and friends.

Your sense of sight also helps to keep you safe and allows you to find your way around. Your eyes check for traffic before you cross the road and they prevent you from tripping over or bumping into things.

DID YOU KNOW?
About two-thirds of the information your brain receives comes from what you see.

Your eyes are like a window on the world. They let you enjoy hundreds of different experiences, such as observing animals, looking at beautiful flowers, seeing famous places, or watching a football match.

As you read, your eyes move rapidly along lines of words and your brain takes in their meaning.

These people are using their eyes to look at new and exciting sights around them.

These children are turning their heads to get a good, clear view of the road. They are using their eyes to spot any danger.

5

How your eyes work

YOUR EYES are two rubbery balls. They are the size of ping-pong balls. and sit in bony **eye sockets** in your **skull**. When you turn your head you can look in any direction and see what is going on around you. Your eyes can also move. There are six sets of **muscles** attached to each eye which allow them to swivel up, down, from side to side, or to circle like the hands of a clock.

Each eye is made up of three different layers. At the front is the **cornea**. In the middle are the **pupil**, **iris** and **lens**. At the back are the **retina** and the **optic nerve** which sends messages to your brain. Your eyes are filled with a watery jelly, which helps them to keep their shape.

DID YOU KNOW?
Your eye muscles are very active and move about 100,000 times a day. Many of these movements take place when you are fast asleep!

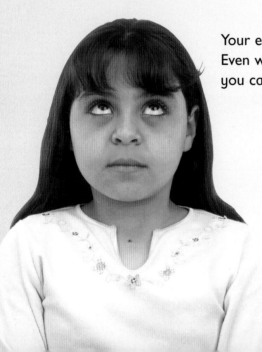
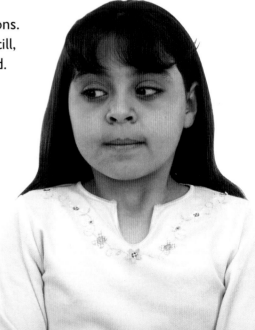

Your eyes can move in all directions. Even when you keep your head still, you can have a good look around.

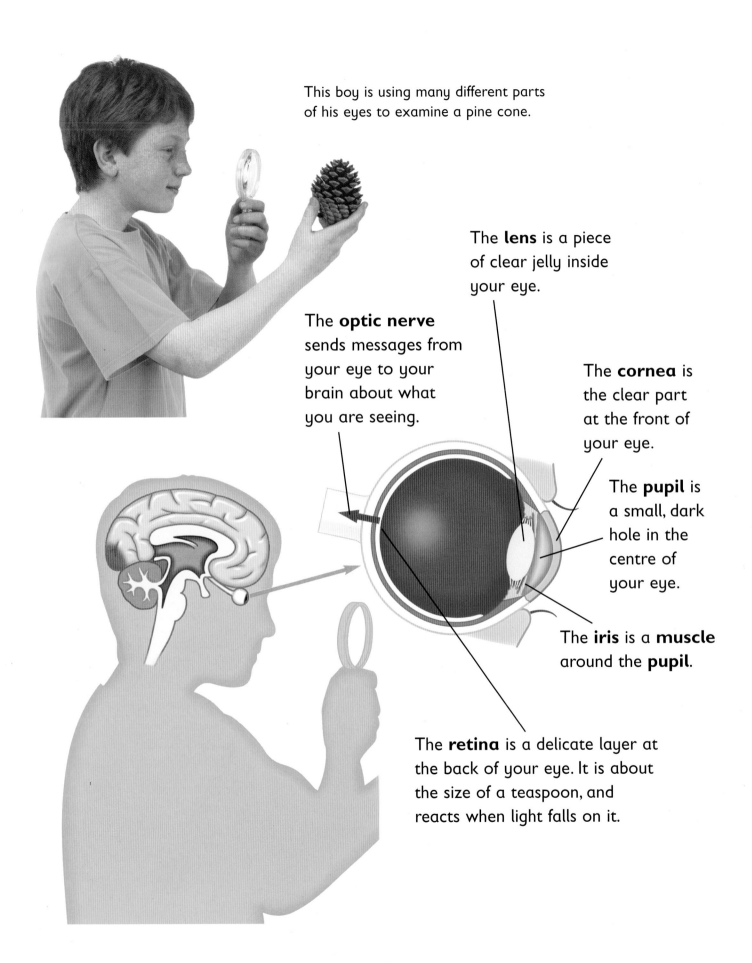

This boy is using many different parts of his eyes to examine a pine cone.

The **lens** is a piece of clear jelly inside your eye.

The **optic nerve** sends messages from your eye to your brain about what you are seeing.

The **cornea** is the clear part at the front of your eye.

The **pupil** is a small, dark hole in the centre of your eye.

The **iris** is a **muscle** around the **pupil**.

The **retina** is a delicate layer at the back of your eye. It is about the size of a teaspoon, and reacts when light falls on it.

Letting in light

YOU NEED light to be able to see. The light passes through the **cornea** at the front of your eye and enters a hole called the **pupil**. The size of the pupil changes to control how much light enters your eye.

In bright light, the pupil shrinks to a pinprick to prevent the **retina** from being damaged by too much light. When it is dim, the pupil opens wider to let in more light.

The pupil does not change size by itself. It is controlled by a **muscle** called the **iris**. When the iris tightens, the pupil gets smaller. When the iris relaxes, the pupil gets bigger again.

STAY HEALTHY
Your retina is very delicate and can be damaged by the sun. Wearing sunglasses and a cap will protect your eyes from harmful rays. This is especially important if you spend a lot of time outside.

DID YOU KNOW?
Your pupils grow bigger when you are angry or afraid. They get smaller when you feel relaxed.

You inherit the colour of your irises from your parents. What colour are yours?

8

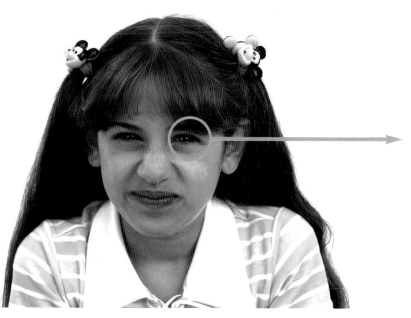

The **iris** tightens in bright sunlight.

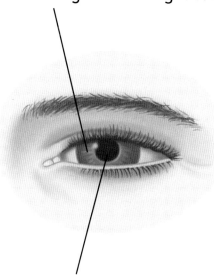

The **pupil** gets smaller and less light reaches the **retina** at the back of your eye.

Bright light can be uncomfortable. It can make you crease up your eyes, and squint.

In the shade, you can open your eyes wider.

When you put a sunhat on to shade your eyes, the iris relaxes.

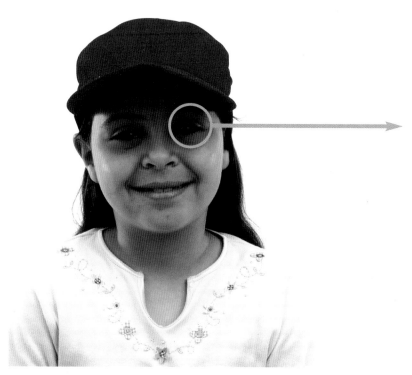

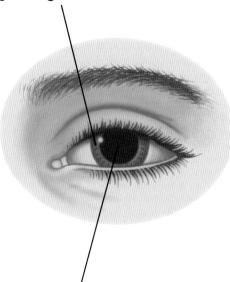

The pupil gets larger to let in more light.

Forming a picture

Y OUR EYES work like a camera. They 'take a picture' through a **lens** just like a camera does. Inside your eye, the picture is stored on the **retina** – a bit like a picture that is stored on a reel of film.

The lens in your eye is a small piece of jelly, just behind each of your **pupils**. Whenever you look at things around you, light bounces off the objects and into your eyes. The lens in each eye **focuses** this light so that it falls on the retina, and forms an upside-down picture. The retina reacts by sending messages to the brain. The brain sorts out these messages and allows you to see the picture the right way up.

DID YOU KNOW?
A newborn baby sees the world upside-down. It is several months before a baby's brain learns to turn pictures the right way up.

Vitamin A helps the retina to work properly. It is found in foods such as liver, green vegetables, milk, cheese, butter and eggs.

When you look at an object, your eyes and brain work together to tell you what you are seeing.

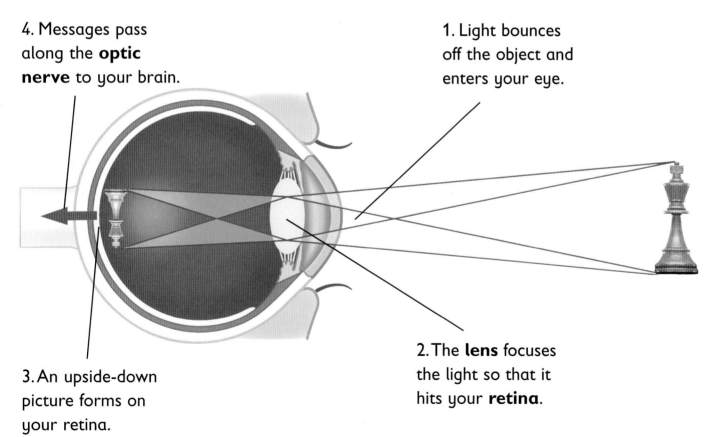

4. Messages pass along the **optic nerve** to your brain.

1. Light bounces off the object and enters your eye.

3. An upside-down picture forms on your retina.

2. The **lens** focuses the light so that it hits your **retina**.

Seeing close and far

TRY LOOKING at something close up (like the fingers of your hand) and then at something further away. You will find that you can't **focus** on both things at the same time. A camera can take pictures of objects that are close up or far away by moving the camera **lens** backwards or forwards. Your eye does this by changing the shape of the lens itself.

When you look at objects that are far away, the lens becomes thin and flat. When you look at things that are close up, the lens becomes fat and rounded. In each case, the shape of the lens helps to focus the light so that it falls on the **retina** and forms a clear picture. As you look around, the lens is always changing shape. It can do this quickly and easily because it is very elastic.

As you grow older, the lenses in your eyes grow tougher and change shape more slowly. That is why it takes longer for elderly people to focus on things.

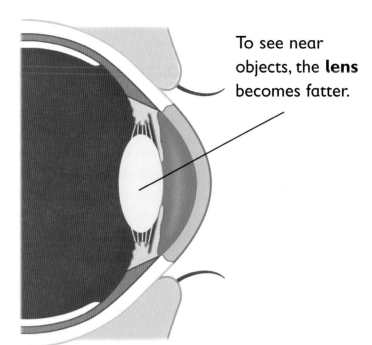

To see near objects, the **lens** becomes fatter.

The lenses in your eyes change shape depending on whether you are looking at something near or far from you. However, your eye cannot focus on anything closer than 15 cm in front of you.

To see distant objects, the lens becomes thinner.

DID YOU KNOW?
Your eyes always work together. It takes quite an effort to make your eyes work separately, such as when you go cross-eyed!

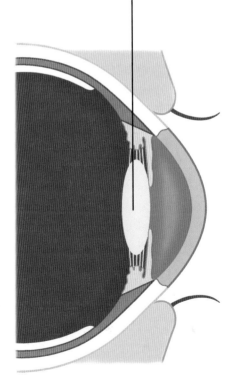

Seeing in colour

L IGHT IS made up of many different colours. You can see these colours because the **retina** reacts to them in different ways. So, when you look at a tomato, only certain parts of the retina react to the colour red. These parts send messages to the brain to say that the tomato is red.

Sometimes the retina does not work properly, and people cannot see all the colours. These people are said to be **colour-blind**. The most common colour-blindness is not being able to tell red from green. True colour-blindness, when you cannot see any colours at all, is very rare.

Colour is one of the first things we notice about an object. This is why sports teams wear different-coloured clothes, so that players can instantly pick out their team-mates.

DID YOU KNOW?
Colour-blindness can be dangerous. That is why traffic signals never rely on green and red colours alone. They always follow the same sequence, so even if you cannot see the colours, you know when it is safe to go.

Different parts of the retina respond to different colours. It helps this boy to tell what colour he is looking at.

When you look at a red ball the parts of your **retina** that react to the colour red 'wake up'.

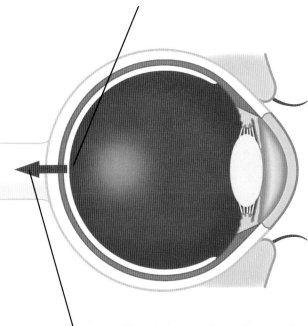

A message is sent to your brain along the **optic nerve**.

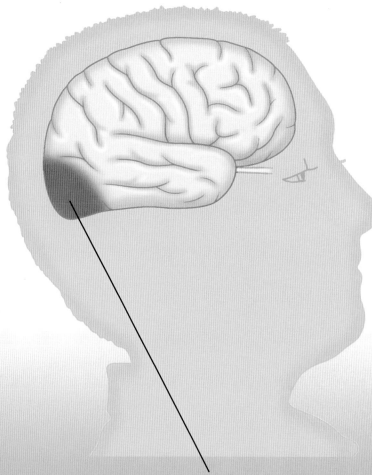

The vision part of your brain identifies the colour you have seen as red.

When it is hard to see

I T IS hard to see in the dark, but your eyes can adjust to darkness. The **pupils** open as wide as they can to let in as much light as possible. Your eyes also make a special chemical that helps to boost the **retina**. The chemical takes a while to work, but after ten to twenty minutes in darkness you can see much more clearly.

It is also hard to see when you are underwater. If you open your eyes in water, everything looks blurry. To see clearly, light has to pass through air before it enters your eyes. That is why swimmers wear goggles and divers wear masks. These provide an air-space between the water and their eyes, helping them to **focus**.

Swimming goggles help you to see underwater. In swimming pools they also protect your eyes from chlorine, which can make them red and sore.

Riding a bike at night can be dangerous. Cyclists use lights and wear reflectors on their clothes so that drivers can see them more clearly.

Brightly-coloured clothes make a cyclist more visible during the daytime and at night.

Reflective strips shine brightly, especially in car headlights.

A white light at the front of a bike and a red light at the back show drivers which direction the bike is travelling in.

A trick of the eye

SOMETIMES YOU can be tricked into seeing things. For instance, your eyes are tricked every time you go to the cinema. You think you are seeing pictures moving on the screen, but a reel of film is made up of thousands of photographs. How is it they seem to move?

The pictures appear to move because they pass through a projector very quickly. Your eyes are too slow to see each one move separately, and so your brain joins the pictures together.

STAY HEALTHY

When you watch television, make sure the room is well lit, and try not to watch in the dark. The flickering images can damage your eyes. Sit at least two metres away from the television and rest your eyes every now and then by looking away from the screen.

Pictures can move through a projector at a speed of 24 pictures a second. This is too fast for your eyes to see each individual picture.

DID YOU KNOW?

Photographs are made up of tiny dots of colour. Look closely at a newspaper photo and you will see the dots. Your brain joins these dots together so that they seem to make a solid colour.

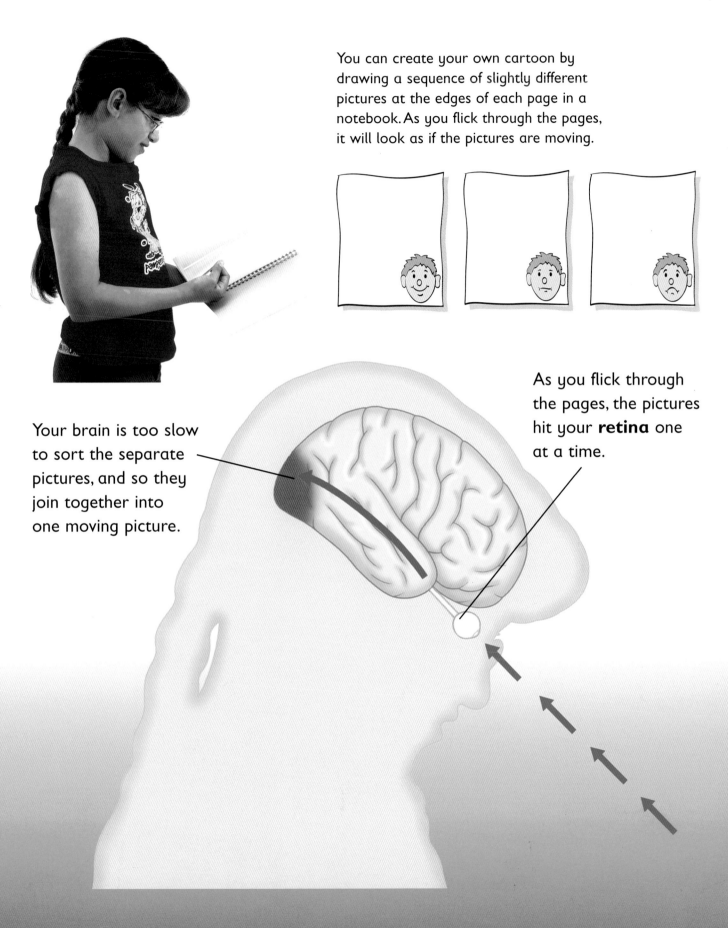

You can create your own cartoon by drawing a sequence of slightly different pictures at the edges of each page in a notebook. As you flick through the pages, it will look as if the pictures are moving.

As you flick through the pages, the pictures hit your **retina** one at a time.

Your brain is too slow to sort the separate pictures, and so they join together into one moving picture.

Protecting your eyes

YOUR EYES are soft and fragile, so they need protecting from harm. This is why they sit inside a bony hole called the **eye socket** which protects them from knocks and bumps.

They also need to be kept clean. So you have eyebrows and eyelashes to stop sweat and dirt entering your eyes.

Your **eyelids** help to keep your eyes clean and moist. Every time you blink, a salty liquid washes across your eyes, wiping away any **germs** or dust. If something larger gets into your eye, it produces salty tears which wash the intruder away.

Many people do jobs that could harm their eyes. This welder is wearing a transparent mask to protect his eyes from burning sparks.

STAY HEALTHY
Eyelids cannot protect your eyes against every kind of danger. Always wear safety goggles if you are doing anything that might hurt them, such as using chemicals in a science lesson.

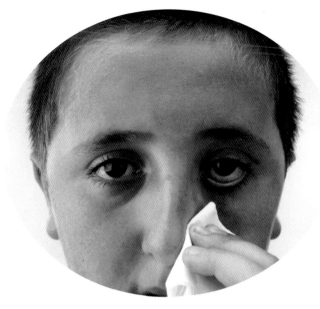

This boy has some dirt in his eye which is making it water. He is using a handkerchief to wipe away the tears.

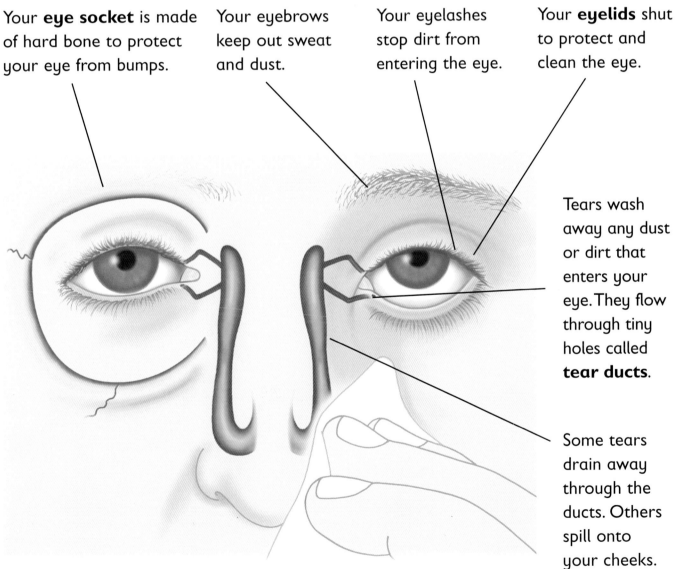

Your **eye socket** is made of hard bone to protect your eye from bumps.

Your eyebrows keep out sweat and dust.

Your eyelashes stop dirt from entering the eye.

Your **eyelids** shut to protect and clean the eye.

Tears wash away any dust or dirt that enters your eye. They flow through tiny holes called **tear ducts**.

Some tears drain away through the ducts. Others spill onto your cheeks.

How animals see

EVERY ANIMAL depends on its **senses** to survive, but different animals depend on different senses. An eagle has excellent eyesight because it hunts from the sky. A mole, which lives in dark tunnels, can hardly see at all.

Night-hunters, such as cats and owls, can see well in the dark. They have large eyes to help them take in a lot of light. This enables them to hunt on the darkest nights when they cannot be seen by their prey.

For an animal, having good eyesight can mean the difference between life and death. Some animals, such as rabbits and antelope, have eyes on the sides of their heads. This helps them to spot danger all around them. Hunters, like eagles, have eyes that sit at the front of their head so they can focus more easily on their prey.

DID YOU KNOW?
A fly's eyes are made up of hundreds of pieces. Each one contains a tiny lens that sees just part of a scene. The fly has to put all the pieces together to see the whole picture.

Part of the eagle's eye is like a magnifying glass. This helps it to zoom in on small animals that are hidden on the ground.

A cat's large eyes give it excellent vision both in darkness and in light.

A cat's eyes are forward-facing to **focus** on prey. They also help the cat to judge distances so that it can pounce accurately.

At night, the **pupil** opens very wide to collect as much light as possible.

By day, the pupil is a narrow slit to stop too much light entering.

How glasses work

MANY PEOPLE have problems with their sight. This is usually because the **lens** cannot **focus** light onto the **retina** properly, and so it blurs the picture they see. Glasses or **contact lenses** help to correct this.

Some people can see distant objects easily, but close objects appear blurred. These people are said to be **long-sighted**. Other people can see close objects clearly, but distant objects are blurred. These people are **short-sighted**. Each group needs a different kind of lens to correct the problem. Glasses and **contact lenses** work in similar ways: they create an extra lens that bends the light before it enters the eye and focuses it on the retina properly.

DID YOU KNOW?
There are also lenses in magnifying glasses, telescopes, binoculars, microscopes, cameras, CD players, photocopiers and medical instruments.

Lenses are used inside many scientific instruments. The lenses in this microscope make tiny things look bigger so that they can be studied closely.

Without glasses, light **focuses** behind the **retina**, and the image that forms is blurred.

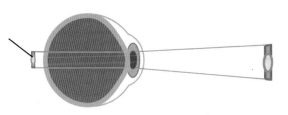

With a **convex lens** the light bends and focuses on the retina. Now the girl can tell what the time is.

A convex lens is thicker in the middle than at the edge.

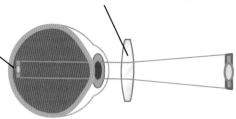

This girl is long-sighted, which means she cannot focus on close objects, like the face of a watch. So she wears glasses with convex lenses.

Without glasses, light focuses in front of the retina and the image is blurred.

This boy is short-sighted, which means he cannot focus on distant objects, such as a picture across a room. So he wears glasses with concave lenses.

A concave lens is thinner in the middle than at the edge.

With a **concave lens**, light focuses on the retina. Now the picture is clear.

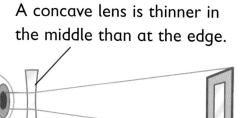

Being blind

B LIND PEOPLE are unable to see. Some people are born blind, but others become blind after an illness or injury, or because of old age. Only a very few blind people see nothing at all. Most have some sight, even if it is only shadowy. They use this along with their other **senses**, such as hearing, smell and touch, to perform everyday tasks.

Most blind people are able to lead very independent lives. Some have guide dogs, which help them to find their way around. The dog and its owner are good companions and work together as a team. The guide dog helps its owner to get on and off buses, cross roads and do many other activities.

DID YOU KNOW?
A Braille reader can read up to 400 words a minute. That's as fast as a good reader reading print.

Blind people learn to read using an alphabet called **Braille**. In Braille, raised dots stand for letters, numbers, commas and full stops.

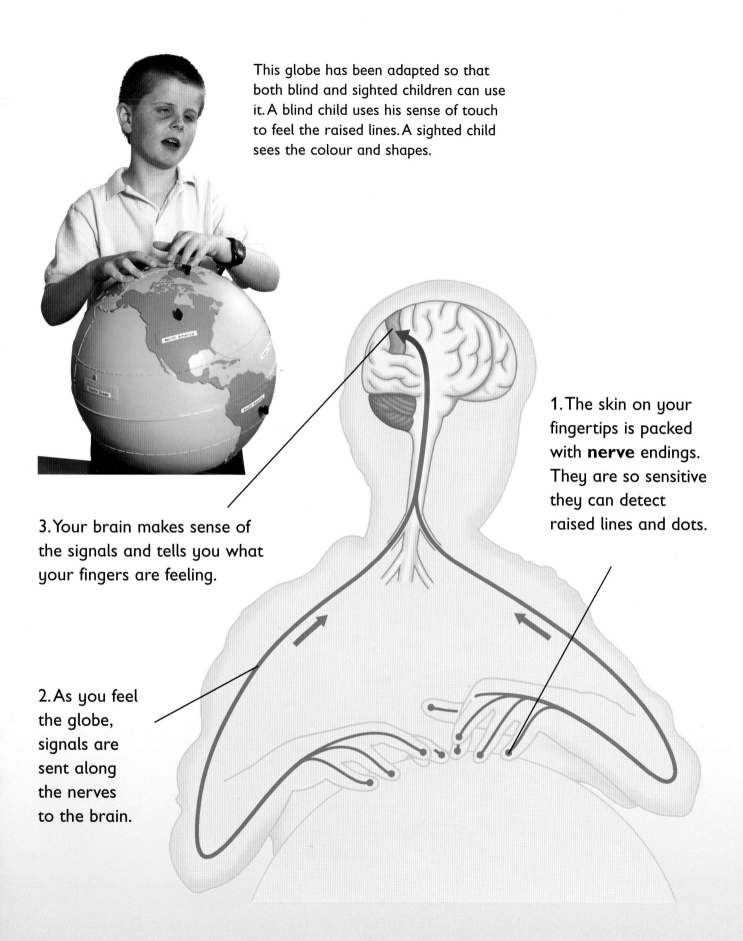

This globe has been adapted so that both blind and sighted children can use it. A blind child uses his sense of touch to feel the raised lines. A sighted child sees the colour and shapes.

1. The skin on your fingertips is packed with **nerve** endings. They are so sensitive they can detect raised lines and dots.

3. Your brain makes sense of the signals and tells you what your fingers are feeling.

2. As you feel the globe, signals are sent along the nerves to the brain.

Caring for your eyes

TO KEEP your eyes healthy, you need to eat a balanced diet made up of many different foods. You should also have your eyes tested every year by an **optician**. Opticians are eye experts who carry out a number of tests. First, they shine a bright light into each eye. This helps them to see inside the eye and check that the **retina**, **blood vessels** and **optic nerve** are all healthy.

The beam of an optician's torch lights up the inside of the eye. This allows him to check for problems or disease.

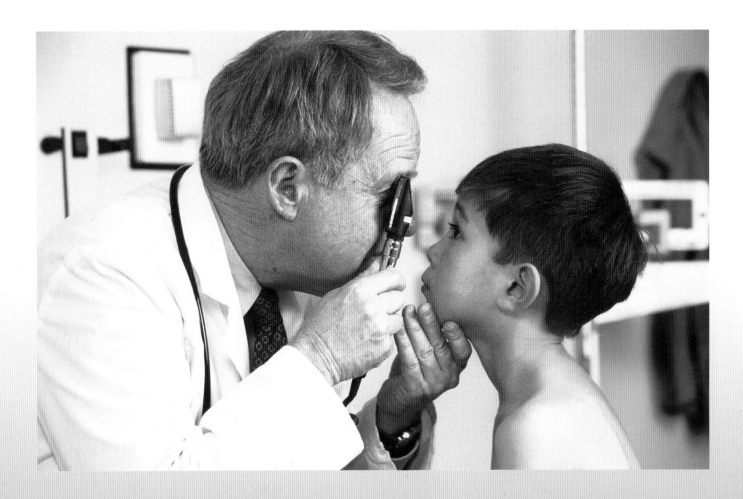

200 ft. or 61 m.

E

100 ft. or 30.5 m.

C B

70 ft. or 21.75 m.

D L F

50 ft. or 15.24 m.

P T E O

40 ft. or 12.19 m.

F Z B D E

30 ft. or 9.14 m.

O F L C T B

20 ft. or 6.10 m.

T P E O L F D Z

15 ft. or 4.75 m.

L P C T Z B D F E O

10 ft. or 3.05 m.

Z O C E F L D P B T

DID YOU KNOW?
Some medical conditions, such as **diabetes**, cause changes in the eye. This means that opticians may notice the signs of diabetes before people even know they have it.

Most people can see the largest letters on the optician's chart, but the smallest ones may not be clear.

Next, the optician checks that your eyes are **focusing** properly by asking you to read some letters on a chart. First you read them with both eyes. Then you cover up one eye at a time, and read the letters with the other eye. This tests whether one eye is better than the other. The results of these tests tell the optician whether or not you need glasses.

STAY HEALTHY
Contact lenses need careful cleaning, otherwise they may spread **infection**. Clean them every day with a disinfecting solution. Never wipe them with a wet finger.

Glossary

blood vessels The tubes through which blood flows.

Braille A system of writing which allows blind people to read by touch. Each letter is a different pattern of raised dots.

colour-blindness A condition which prevents people seeing the difference between certain colours – for example, between red and green.

concave lens A lens that is thinner in the middle than at the edge. It helps short-sighted people to see distant objects clearly.

contact lens A very small, thin lens which fits over the eye to improve a person's sight.

convex lens A lens that is thicker in the middle than at the edge. It helps long-sighted people to see near objects clearly.

cornea A clear layer at the front of the eye.

diabetes An illness that stops the body from controlling the amount of sugar in the blood. It can cause eye problems.

eye socket A circle of hard bone which surrounds and protects each eye.

eyelid The fold of skin and muscle that can be closed to cover each eye.

focus To form a clear picture.

germ A very small living thing that can enter your body and cause disease.

infection A disease or illness that can spread from one person to another.

iris The ring of muscle that forms the round, coloured part of the eye.

lens The piece of clear jelly inside the eye which focuses light onto the retina.

long-sighted When people cannot see close objects clearly they are long-sighted.

muscle Tissues that can move different parts of the body.

nerves Bundles of fibres that carry signals between the brain and other parts of the body.

optic nerve The nerve that carries signals between the eye and the brain.

optician An eye expert who examines people's eyes, and can provide glasses or contact lenses to improve their sight.

pupil The small, round opening at the front of the eye that lets in light.

reflector Something shiny that reflects light and gleams in the dark when light falls on it.

retina The layer at the back of the eye which reacts to light and sends messages to the brain.

senses The five senses - sight, hearing, taste, smell and touch - give us information about the world around us and help to protect us.

short-sighted When people cannot see distant objects clearly they are short-sighted.

skull The bones that protect your brain.

tear duct A tiny hole in the corner of each eye through which tears flow.

vitamin A A substance found in food, which our body needs in tiny amounts to work properly. There are many other vitamins, such as vitamin C and D.

Useful information

Books

How Do Our Eyes See? Carol Ballard, from the "How Our Bodies Work" series (Wayland, 1997)

Looking Brenda Walpole, from the "See for Yourself" series (A & C Black, 1996)

Being Blind Peter White, from the "Think About" series (Belitha Press, 1998)

Senses Anna Sandeman, from the "Your Body" series (Watts, 2000)

Senses Steve Parker, from the "Look at Your Body" series (Watts, 1996)

Websites

www.sciencemuseum.org.uk/on-line/outofsight/index.asp
Information and experiments about optical illusions.

www.grand-illusions.com/index.htm
A good site for older readers with many interesting optical illusions.

http://members.tripod.com/manisha_b/
Lots of information, pictures, tips and fun facts about seeing.

Organisations

Royal National Institute for the Blind
224 Great Portland Street
London
W1N 6AA
Tel: 020 7391 2397
www.rnib.org.uk

Index